C000010840

Queens of the Tyne

The River's Great Liners 1888-1973

The Cunard Liner "MAURETANIA"

Ken Smith

Tyne Bridge Publishing

Acknowledgements

The author would like to thank the following for their kind help in the preparation of this book: Brian Aitken, Editor, *The Journal*, Newcastle; Colin Boyd and Liz Rees, Tyne & Wear Archives Service; Ken Heslewood; Ray Marshall; PricewaterhouseCoopers; Ian Whitehead, Tyne & Wear Museums.

Illustrations acknowledgements: TWAS: Tyne & Wear Archives Service; Cunard; Ken Heslewood Collection; ncjMedia; National Museums Liverpool (Merseyside Maritime Museum); University of Liverpool Library. Unless otherwise indicated illustrations are from the collections of Newcastle Libraries & Information Service.
Every endeavour has been taken to trace copyright holders of the images in this publication.

© Ken Smith, 2007

Published by
City of Newcastle upon Tyne
Newcastle Libraries & Information Service
Tyne Bridge Publishing
2007

www.tynebridgepublishing.co.uk

Tyne Bridge Publishing
Newcastle Libraries
PO Box 88
Newcastle upon Tyne
NE99 1DX

ISBN 978 1 85795 113 4

A free catalogue featuring our wide range of local and maritime history publications is available.

Front cover:

There she goes! Workmen look on as the *Reina Victoria-Eugenia* is launched at Swan Hunter & Wigham Richardson's Neptune Yard, Low Walker, Newcastle, on 26 September, 1912. Completed the following year, this Spanish passenger liner was built for the Cia Transatlantica, of Barcelona, and served mainly on the run between Spain, Cuba and Mexico.

With a gross tonnage of 10,137, the *Reina Victoria-Eugenia* was a small liner, although at the time of her maiden voyage in 1913 she was Spain's largest passenger ship. The vessel was sunk by aircraft attack during the Spanish Civil War in 1939. *(TWAS, Swan Hunter Archive)*

Back cover:

The Tyne-built liner *Mauretania* at Liverpool, c. 1910. *(Ken Heslewood Collection)*

Dominion Monarch enters the Tyne for a refit, 1953.

Contents

The Speed Queen   5

Troops and Cruises   16

Compassion on the Sea   22

Rescue at Dawn   28

A Trio of Monarchs   36

The Pride of Norway   46

The Empress   52

An Unlucky Star   60

Rescued and Bombed   64

The Last Queen   68

Index of ships   72

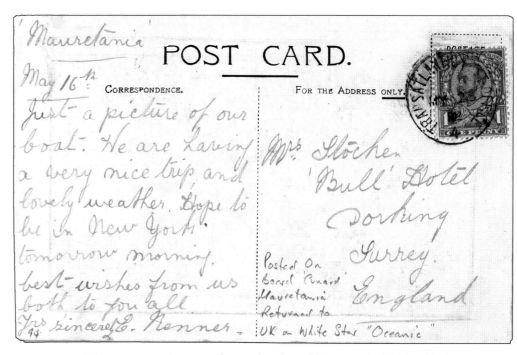

Written at sea. A postcard posted on board Mauretania 16 May 1912.

Ken Heslewood Collection

Welcome home! Mauretania is greeted by crowds as she re-enters the Tyne in 1921 for conversion to oil-firing from coal.

The Speed Queen

Cunard's *Mauretania*, completed in 1907, was without doubt the most famous passenger ship built on the Tyne. She stands out above all other liners launched from the banks of this famed North-East river. She was a Tyne icon long before the advent of inspiring structures such as the superbly designed Tyne Bridge and Gateshead Millennium Bridge.

Mauretania sailed on her maiden voyage across the Atlantic nearly five years before the *Titanic* sailed on her ill-fated maiden passage and sank with great loss of life after striking an iceberg. The Tyne's greatest liner had one or two narrow escapes in her career but she survived the First World War and won the affections of nearly all who sailed in her.

There were, however, some similarities between these two huge vessels. Both had passenger accommodation which reflected the rigid class structure of the early 1900s. First-, second- and third- (steerage) class travellers were segregated aboard ship, living in different worlds, much as they did when ashore. Both ships also bore four tall funnels – conveying an image of speed, power and prestige. In an era when the aeroplane was in its infancy travellers were totally reliant on ships to travel from Europe to the United States or anywhere else overseas. Ships were therefore of immense importance. The fastest vessels with the best accommodation and facilities as well as impressive looks attracted the most lucrative business upon the Atlantic.

It was also understandably an advantage for a shipping line's vessels to be seen as strong on safety measures. Intriguingly, *Mauretania* was billed at the time of her maiden voyage as nearly unsinkable, but not, it seems, by Cunard. An advertisement in a special edition of *The Shipbuilder* magazine in 1907 stated: 'The *Mauretania* is practically unsinkable owing to the watertight bulkhead doors hydraulically controlled by the Stone Lloyd System.' Similar sentiments were to be expressed about the *Titanic* in 1912.

Despite the similarities, *Mauretania* was the faster ship, her engines generating 68,000 horsepower as opposed to *Titanic*'s 51,000. The Tyne's best loved liner was built to be a speed queen.

Mauretania was launched into the Tyne at the Wallsend Shipyard of Swan Hunter & Wigham Richardson Ltd on 20 September 1906. Her debut marked the birth of a legend. She was to become an emblem of the pride, skill and energy of Tyneside workmanship.

The ship, at 31,938 gross tons the largest liner built on the Tyne, went on to hold the coveted Blue Riband for the fastest crossing of the North Atlantic longer than any other ship in the first half of the 20th century and was undoubtedly one of the most successful passenger vessels of her era.

Mauretania was born out of British national pride as much as commercial considerations. Along with her sister, the ill-fated *Lusitania*, she was the United Kingdom's answer to the German liners which had held the Blue Riband during the ten years preceding her maiden voyage in 1907.

In 1903 the British government and Cunard agreed that two large, fast passenger ships should be built to win back the Blue Riband for Britain and re-establish her supremacy on the flourishing crossing to New York. Under the terms of the agreement, which was ratified by Parliament, the government agreed to loan Cunard £2.6 million for the building of the two ships. On top of this, it was to grant the company an annual subsidy of £150,000 towards the upkeep of the vessels, which were to carry the mails.

However, important conditions were attached to this financial aid. It was stipulated that the two liners would have to maintain a speed of between 24 and 25 knots in moderate weather and that the ships would be made available as armed auxiliary cruisers in time of war. In addition, Cunard was required to remain a British company and all the ships' officers as well as the majority of their seamen were required to be British.

The order for one of the ships, *Mauretania*, was placed with Swan Hunter & Wigham Richardson of Wallsend, and the other, *Lusitania*, with John Brown of Clydebank.

Before work could begin on building the vessels careful planning was needed to ensure as far as possible that they would be the fastest liners upon the prestigious North Atlantic run. Cunard therefore appointed a special commission of experts to inquire into what would be the best type of engine to capture the Riband. After a great deal of study, the commission eventually decided that the rela-

Charles Parsons

Andrew Laing

tively new turbine engine, the invention of Tyneside engineering genius Charles Parsons, should be chosen.

Two Tyneside companies, C.S. Swan and Hunter, of the Wallsend Shipyard, and Wigham Richardson, of the Neptune Shipyard, Low Walker, merged in 1903 to combine their resources to bid for the *Mauretania* contract. Swan and Hunter was no stranger to Cunard. Its slipways had already seen the launch of two intermediate-sized Cunard passenger liners, *Ivernia* and *Carpathia*. The standard of its designs and workmanship had clearly impressed the shipping line. The firm resulting from the merger, Swan Hunter & Wigham Richardson Ltd., was thus by no means an unknown quantity and after submission of various designs it won the lucrative order to build the ship.

The contract for the powerful turbine engines of *Mauretania* went to the Wallsend Slipway and Engineering Co. Ltd., of Willington Quay, Wallsend. The giant turbine machinery of *Mauretania* was the firm's greatest challenge to date. The management and workforce of Wallsend Slipway and Engineering were to prove highly successful in meeting this challenge. Behind their success, however, stood Charles Parsons, the inventor of the steam turbine engine, whose brilliance and ingenuity were the ultimate reasons for the great liner's speed achievements.

The manager of Wallsend Slipway and Engineering at this time was Andrew Laing. It was Laing who led the talented team which had the task of designing the engines according to the principles developed by Parsons. They brilliantly adapted those

The Blue Riband

The prestigious Blue Riband for the fastest crossing of the North Atlantic by a passenger vessel was first awarded in the 19th century when leading shipping companies informally agreed that a blue riband could be flown from the mast of the winner. However, until 1935, when British MP Sir Harold Hales provided a trophy, the honour existed in name only, apart from the right to fly the riband. The honour can be captured separately for the westbound and eastbound crossings between Europe and America. It is based on the average speed achieved by a vessel on the passage, not on the time taken. Winning the Riband in the heyday of passenger liners was a prize of great value to a shipping company since the successful vessel would boost its attraction to passengers.

The first ship to be generally recognised as holding the Blue Riband was the pioneering steamer *Sirius* which crossed the North Atlantic from Cork to New York in 18 days, 10 hours, at an average speed of 6.7 knots in 1838. She was closely followed, only a few hours later, by the *Great Western*, which crossed from Avonmouth to New York in 15 days, 10.5 hours, at an average of 8.7 knots. She was thus the second holder of the Riband. The *Great Western* cut the crossing time down to 13 days, 6 hours, in 1839 at an average of 9.6 knots.

The Tyne-built *Mauretania* and her Clyde-built sister *Lusitania* were the first passenger liners to cross the Atlantic in under five days. On her maiden voyage in 1907 *Mauretania* captured the Blue Riband for the eastern crossing with an average speed of 23.69 knots. The passage from the Ambrose Light, New York, to Queenstown (now Cobh), Ireland, took 4 days, 22 hours, 29 minutes. In 1909 *Mauretania* took the westward honour with an average speed of 26.06 knots between the Daunt's Rock and Sandy Hook. This passage took 4 days, 10 hours, 51 minutes.

Among other illustrious liners to hold the record were the *Bremen*, of Germany, Italy's *Rex,* the *Normandie*, of France, and Britain's famed *Queen Mary*. The last conventional passenger liner to win the Blue Riband was America's *United States*. In 1952, she won the honour with a passage from the Ambrose Light, New York, to the Bishop's Rock, off Cornwall, England, with an average speed of 35.59 knots. The *United States* had crossed in 3 days, 10 hours, 40 minutes.

However, even this record was to be surpassed. In 1990, the powerful catamaran *Hoverspeed Great Britain* won the honour. Then in 1998, the Danish catamaran, *Cat-Link V*, a large car and passenger ferry driven by diesel engines, crossed from New York to the Bishop's Rock in 2 days, 20 hours, 9 minutes, thus capturing the Blue Riband and the Hales Trophy. Her average speed was an amazing 41.284 knots. The vessel was later renamed *Master Cat*. She had beaten a record set by another catamaran, *Catalonia*, only a month earlier. All three catamarans had been built in Australia by the Incat company.

principles to *Mauretania*'s require-ments. This involved constructing the largest turbine engines to be installed in any ship up to that date, under licence from the Parsons company.

The keel of *Mauretania* was laid down at Swan Hunter & Wigham Richardson's Wallsend Shipyard in 1904. The great liner was built on a berth inside a huge shed constructed of metal girders and posts. This shed was more than 130ft high and over 700ft long. It featured a glazed roof which enabled building to proceed in virtually all weathers and arc lamps were provided to allow work on the

TWAS, Swan Hunter Archive

Mauretania's framework takes shape in her enormous shed at the Wallsend Shipyard on 4 April 1905.

berth at night. The roof girders were fitted with electric over-head cranes.

The giant ship which took shape at Wallsend had an overall length of 790ft and a maximum beam of 88ft. She was driven by four huge propellers, each with three and later four blades, linked directly to her turbine engines, which were placed under the waterline. Equipped with twenty-five boilers and 192 coal-burning furnaces, the ship needed 324 firemen and trimmers to man the stokehold.

By September 1906 *Mauretania* was ready for her launch, after which she would be moved by tugs to her fitting-out mooring alongside the yard. Two large dolphins (mooring structures) had been sited in the river for this purpose. Other preparations included special dredging operations to ensure adequate water depth.

The launch ceremony was performed on 20 September 1906 by the Dowager Duchess of Roxburghe, whose brother-in-law was the First Lord of the Admiralty. Not surprisingly, thousands of onlookers crowded the banks of the Tyne at Wallsend and Hebburn. The shipyard itself was also packed with spectators. They were entertained by the 1st Newcastle Artillery Band.

Christening the ship *Mauretania*, the name for the ancient Roman province of north west Africa, the Dowager Duchess broke a bottle of wine over the liner's bows. As the ship began to move towards the Tyne, steamers sounded their sirens, adding to the cheers of the crowds. She entered the water only forty seconds after

starting her journey. The *Mauretania* was born.

There was only one accident reported during the launch. A workman was slightly injured when a piece of glass from the shattered wine bottle fell on his head. However, he was quickly given first aid and was said to be little worse for his experience.

After her launch, six tugs towed *Mauretania* to her near-

TWAS, Swan Hunter Archive

Under the giant. Workmen pose under one of the four huge propellers. Initially each of these propellers had three blades. In 1909 the number of blades was increased to four on each propeller and the liner's speed performance improved.

by fitting-out mooring where she would receive her funnels, engines, and boilers and where work on her cabins, public rooms and a host of other details would be carried out.

The fitting-out of the liner took just over one year and represented a tremendous feat of labour by the workers of the Wallsend Shipyard. The boilers and other heavy machinery, including the six turbines, were lowered into the ship by a large floating crane, the *Titan*, capable of lifting 150 tons.

On 17 September 1907, as the vessel neared completion, she was taken down the Tyne to the North Sea for preliminary trials which lasted five days. Large crowds flocked to the river's banks to see *Mauretania* put to sea for the first time. On her journey down river she was towed and guided by the Dutch tugs *Ocean* and *Poolzee* and the South Shields tugs *Snowdon* and *Washington*.

Ken Heslewood Collection

Birth of a legend. This postcard shows Mauretania's launch on 20 September 1906.

During her test runs the liner's speed performance was encouraging. She achieved a maximum of 27.75 knots and averaged over 26 knots while steaming between St Abb's Head in Berwickshire and Flamborough Head, Yorkshire. Carrier pigeons were released from the ship to take news of the progress of the trials to the Wallsend Shipyard.

On 21 September the vessel returned to the Tyne. A month later all was ready. *Mauretania* had taken two years, five months to build from the signing of the full contract in 1905. At the date of her completion she was the largest ship

of any description to be launched on the river, and the liner was truly the pride of Tyneside. An army of Geordie workmen had poured all their energy and skill into her creation.

It must have been a proud occasion for them when the ship was thrown open to the public for viewing on 12 October. Those who wished to look around the vessel paid two shillings and sixpence and the proceeds went to local charities.

On the afternoon of 22 October 1907 the great ship departed the river of her birth for delivery to Cunard in Liverpool and for her official trials. Tens of thousands of cheering people crowded the Tyne's banks as the tugs

Waterborne at last! The ship with the knife-edged bow enters the water. Her entry into the Tyne was slowed by 1,000 tons of drag chains.

TWAS, Swan Hunter Archive

Snowdon, *President*, *Washington* and *Gauntlet* moved and guided her down to the open sea. The passage took eighty minutes and all went smoothly.

The sirens of the many small boats and the hooters of shipyards and engine works sounded out a salute to the huge vessel. As she left the river those who waved her farewell could not have realised that this four-funnel queen from Wallsend was on course for a career of unparalleled success.

Mauretania steamed northwards around Scotland on her delivery voyage. She was in no rush but still managed an average speed of 22 knots. The liner reached the Canada Dock, Liverpool, on the morning of 24 October. Before her maiden voyage, however, she had to undergo her official trials, which took place in the Irish Sea and the Firth of Clyde during early November. On one run she achieved an impressive 27.36 knots.

Mauretania left Liverpool on her maiden voyage to New York on the evening of November 16 1907. She was under the command of Captain John Pritchard and at that date was the world's largest liner. A cheering crowd of about 50,000 people turned out in wet weather to watch her depart from the Prince's Landing Stage.

Steaming into the night down the Irish Sea, she encountered calm conditions and the following morning reached Queenstown (Cobh), where she took aboard more passengers and mails. She left the Irish port after a two-hour call and glided away into the vast expanse of the North Atlantic.

However, it was not long before the ship

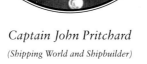

Captain John Pritchard
(*Shipping World and Shipbuilder*)

was to experience her first taste of that ocean's immense power. The liner started to run into the teeth of a westerly gale and soon the winds had reached 50mph. Her bows rose and fell steeply as she met the giant waves head on. Tons of water came crashing on to her foredeck and a spare anchor broke loose. The ship slowed to a mere three knots and her bows were turned away from the wind to enable crewmen, at great risk to themselves, to secure the anchor again. Throughout this procedure she was being violently buffeted by the storm.

Resuming her course, *Mauretania* made good headway despite the rough seas and on the afternoon of the following day conditions began to moderate a little. The damage caused by the storm included broken promenade deck windows, bent railings and water-stained carpets. In defiance of the bad weather, it seemed that she still might achieve a record crossing. Her engines and the men who drove them had performed admirably.

But it was not to be. Fog as well as the storm robbed her of the Blue Riband on her maiden passage westward. This was encountered off Sandy Hook in the approaches to New York. Within hours, however, the fog rapidly lifted and *Mauretania* docked in New York after a crossing lasting five days, 18 hours and 17 minutes. Her speed had averaged between 21 and 22 knots.

On 30 November the ship departed New York on her homeward passage to Liverpool. Fog was again encountered, this time off the

Tyne departure. A splendid atmospheric view on the afternoon of 22 October 1907 as the newly completed Mauretania moves down the Tyne, escorted by tugs, to begin her delivery voyage to Liverpool. She sailed northwards around Scotland to reach her destination. Among those aboard was the chairman of Swan Hunter & Wigham Richardson, George B. Hunter.

Newfoundland Grand Banks, but after a little over a day it cleared and the liner picked up speed, her turbines and stokers working flat out to achieve a record. And this time *Mauretania* carried off what was then the most glittering prize of the seas. She captured the Blue Riband for the eastward crossing with an average speed of 23.69 knots. The passage from the Ambrose Light, New York, to Queenstown, Ireland, had taken four days, 22 hours, 29 minutes.

Ironically, *Mauretania* had wrested the eastward record from her Clyde-built sister, *Lusitania*, rather than a German ship. *Lusitania* had entered service a month earlier and on her second voyage had captured the Riband from the Germans for both westward and eastward crossings. Now, she was forced to give up

Ken Heslewood Collection

Mauretania leaves the Tyne for delivery to Cunard in Liverpool.

the eastward honour to the ship that was the pride of the Tyne. More significantly, however, between them the two British liners now held the record for both directions and had been the first passenger ships to cross the Atlantic in under five days.

In the next few years there followed a friendly contest between the sisters as they vied against each other for the honours. *Mauretania* first gained the westward record in May 1908, steaming across at an average 24.86 knots. But in July of that year *Lusitania* won the westward record back (25.01 knots). However, she never regained the eastward honour from her sister. Also in 1908, one of *Mauretania*'s pro-

pellers was damaged, suffering the loss of a blade. Cunard decided to have a new set of propellers fitted, this time with four instead of three blades. The propellers were manufactured by the Wallsend Slipway and Engineering Company and fitted at the Canada Dock, Liverpool. The new screws made their debut in early 1909 and considerably improved her performance.

The decisive moment came in September 1909 when *Mauretania* re-took the westward honour, achieving an average of 26.06 knots between Daunt's Rock and Sandy Hook. The passage had taken four days, 10 hours, 51 minutes. She was now the champion in both directions and from that date onwards *Mauretania* reigned as the supreme ship. She held on to the Blue Riband for a record length of time, retaining the eastward honour for 22 years and the westward for 20.

In September 1910, exactly a year after recapturing the westward prize, she again clocked up 26.06 knots on the passage to New York. This time she clipped ten minutes off her own time, crossing in four days, 10 hours, 41 minutes.

Soon, her fame was spreading on both sides of the Atlantic. Between early 1909 and late 1911 she made 88 crossings of the Atlantic without undergoing a refit. On most of these runs the ship averaged over 25 knots.

During this period of sustained hard work she also gained a reputation for the reliability of her arrival and departure times. Passengers who travelled aboard her developed a fond affection for the fast and elegant ship from the Tyne which moved through the waves with a grace and dignity few could fail to admire.

TWAS, Swan Hunter Archive

Luxury. A first-class special stateroom on Mauretania's D deck. Fine woods of several varieties and comfortable furnishings were used in cabins of this class, giving a 'home from home' feeling for rich passengers.

Troops and Cruises

During her 28-year lifetime *Mauretania*'s passengers ranged from millionaire businessmen and famous personalities in the luxurious first-class accommodation to poor emigrants in her plain third class, bound westward to seek a better life in the New World. However, in 1922 the United States introduced strict quota limitations on the number of immigrants allowed to enter the country and this naturally led to a steep drop in this type of passenger. The answer was a new 'tourist' class, an attempt to attract those of moderate income who might wish to travel for pleasure rather than business or necessity.

When she entered service, the liner could carry 560 passengers in first class, 475 in second class and 1,300 in third. Her crew numbered 812. The vessel could thus accommodate more than 3,000 people.

The first-class areas of the ship included beautifully decorated public rooms and luxury private staterooms, all containing a wealth of woodwork panelling and elegant furniture. A large amount of the woodwork was manufactured in the joinery department of the Wallsend Shipyard.

The first-class dining saloon featured two storeys, surmounted overall by a dome. Both the upper and lower dining levels were panelled in straw-coloured oak in the style of the French king, Francis I. They displayed fine individual carvings cut back from the face of the solid wood. The interior of the dome was adorned with the signs of the Zodiac. The

TWAS, Swan Hunter Archive

The upper and lower levels of the elegant first-class dining room, with its magnificent dome. The upholstery was in deep pink.

colours used were as rich as the ornamentation. Upholstery was deep pink throughout and the carpet of the lower saloon cerise red. The dining areas could seat a total of 480 passengers.

The first-class lounge, also known as the music room, was in 18th century French style. The panelling, columns and pilasters of the lounge were of mahogany. The wood was polished a rich golden brown, with gilt mouldings and carvings. The lounge was crowned with an oval dome. Such luxury and comfort contrasted with the spartan accommodation in third class.

TWAS, Swan Hunter Archive

The third-class general room. The contrast with the first-class public rooms could hardly be greater.

The Poor and the Wealthy

Third-class passengers in *Mauretania* generally purchased one-way tickets – they were on their way, full of hope, to a new life in the United States and did not intend to return. Before the First World War the minimum third-class fare for a one-way passage was £6 to £7. In contrast, a one-way trip with accommodation in one of the luxury suites for the wealthy might cost around £200.

Class distinction was in evidence even for the toilets. Those for first-class passengers on *Mauretania* were labelled 'Ladies' and 'Gentlemen', in contrast to those in third class which were simply styled 'Male' and 'Female'.

Two 'regal suites' were *Mauretania*'s most expensive private cabins. Each suite contained a drawing room, dining room, two bedrooms, a bathroom and corridor. The drawing and dining rooms of one of the suites were panelled in East India satinwood and fitted with marble mantelpieces. Heating was provided by electric radiators, a state-of-the-art feature for the Edwardian era. Furniture in the Georgian-style bedrooms was made from mahogany. The large amount of wood used for passenger accommodation throughout the ship was a tremendous fire risk, but this was normal for the early 1900s.

During the First World War the Tyne's best-loved passenger ship carried troops and also served as a floating hospital. In the summer of 1915 she made three voyages to the Aegean Sea, taking soldiers to the utterly futile Gallipoli campaign. Later that year she was converted into a hospital ship and returned to the Aegean three more times, on these occasions transporting men wounded at Gallipoli home to Britain.

In 1918 *Mauretania* was again used as a troopship and temporarily renamed HMS *Tuber Rose*. She carried thousands of American soldiers from New York to Liverpool on their way to join the Allied armies on the Western Front. After the war, the liner carried many of those who had survived the conflict back to the United States. The American soldiers nicknamed the liner which took them to safety and peace the 'Maury'. During her troopship days she also transported Canadian soldiers to Europe.

In May 1919 *Mauretania* finished her government service and was restored to her pre-war condition, her woodwork and furnishings being reinstalled. Improvements were made to cabins and the liner was cleaned and painted. However, her engines did not receive a major overhaul and this was soon to show up in her speed performance.

The ship's home port was switched from Liverpool to Southampton, but with her destination remaining New York. Calls were made at Cherbourg on the way. Departing

Ken Heslewood Collection

Mauretania as a floating hospital during World War I. She carried wounded soldiers from Gallipoli in 1915.

Southampton for the first time on 6 March 1920 she averaged just over 21 knots westward. The following month her speed was down to 17.81 knots in the same direction and in May of that year 18.35 knots. For the proud 'Maury', these figures were disappointing. But it was clear that her turbine engines were suffering from the strain and stress of many years' hard work.

It was a fire which finally ended this phase of her career and helped to solve the speed problem. The blaze broke out while she was alongside at Southampton on 25 July 1921, badly damaging first-class cabins amidships and the first-class dining room floor above.

The need to repair the damage prompted Cunard to decide that *Mauretania* should at the same time be converted to burn oil instead of coal. Accordingly, she was sent back to her builders, Swan Hunter & Wigham Richardson, of Wallsend, to have the work carried out.

Crowds flocked to the banks of the Tyne to see her arrival in the river of her birth. The task of repairing her and converting her boiler rooms to oil-firing took around six months. In addition, improvements were made to areas of her passenger accommodation.

Mauretania left the Wallsend Shipyard in March 1922 for her return to Southampton. She was towed down the Tyne stern first by the four tugs *Joseph Crosthwaite*, *Ben Ledi*, *Great Emperor* and *Plover*. The tugs *Washington* and *Conqueror* were on station at her bows. But the great liner did not have to suffer the indignity of leaving the river stern first. She was turned off Tyne Dock, her bows now facing seawards.

Later that month, she re-entered service on the Southampton-Cherbourg-New York run and after several more voyages it became clear that the conversion to oil-firing had helped to improve her speed.

The year 1929 was perhaps the most sad in *Mauretania*'s entire career, yet in another way she proved herself a ship of extraordinary resilience. It was the year in which she lost the Blue Riband to the new German liner *Bremen*.

The Shipyard Magazine, courtesy of TWAS

The liner leaves the mouth of the Tyne after her oil conversion work on 11 March 1922. Now burning oil instead of coal, she was given a new lease of life. Mauretania did not lose the Blue Riband until 1929 when she was beaten by the German liner, Bremen.

The two-funnel *Bremen* and her sister ship *Europa* were built to win back the Atlantic honour for Germany. With her two broad funnels and low, streamlined superstructure, the 51,656-ton *Bremen* was an impressive example of a modern liner. She was equipped with engines of over 100,000 horse-power, as against *Mauretania*'s 68,000, and she was fitted with a bulbous bow, an innovation which helped to increase her speed. However, Cunard did not sit back when faced with the possibility of losing the honour. Modifications were carried out to *Mauretania*'s engines to assist her in dealing with this challenge.

The German ship departed Bremerhaven on her maiden passage to New York in July 1929, immediately capturing the Riband for the westward crossing with an average speed of 27.83 knots between Cherbourg and the Ambrose Light. The time taken was four days, 17 hours, 42 minutes. *Mauretania*'s 26.06 knots record had at last been broken. *Bremen* went on to take the eastward honour with 27.92 knots. But *Mauretania*, by this time known as the 'Grand Old Lady of the Atlantic', did not give up without a fight. Leaving Southampton in August, she crossed to New York at an average speed of 26.9 knots. On the eastward run she clocked up an impressive 27.22 knots. The liner had broken her own record in both directions. It was a remarkable achievement for a ship 22 years old, but the *Bremen* remained the faster liner.

In her last years, *Mauretania* was increasingly used as a cruise ship, and returned to the Mediterranean for these leisurely trips each year between 1925 and 1930. In 1931 the liner undertook several popular weekend cruises from New York to Nassau in the Bahamas. These voyages were dubbed the 'Booze Cruises' because many Americans were taking the

CHURCHMAN'S CIGARETTES

R.M.S. "MAURETANIA"

Ken Heslewood Collection

opportunity to escape prohibition.

From early 1933 until the autumn of 1934 she took passengers on a series of cruises to the West Indies. Her hull was painted white in keeping with her luxury role in a sunny climate. Some called her the 'White Queen'.

But her passenger accommodation had never been fully updated, her relative lack of private bathrooms being a major disadvantage, and Cunard reluctantly made the decision that she should be withdrawn from service.

In May 1935, *Mauretania*'s furnishings and fittings were put up for auction. On 1 July 1935 she departed Southampton on her final voyage to a breaker's yard on the shores of the Firth of Forth. It was a sad moment for all who had grown to love *Mauretania* as the great ship steamed northwards on course for her last destination.

On her voyage to the Firth of Forth to be broken up, the liner stopped off the mouth of the Tyne for nearly half an hour to say farewell to the hard-working people who had built her. They had provided her with a sound hull which had withstood the pounding of many Atlantic storms and with superb engines which had proved their worth time and time again. She was the greatest example of the Tyne's shipbuilding and marine engineering skills.

As the liner drew level with the river mouth, rockets were fired from her bridge in salute to her birthplace. Thousands of people had flocked to the seafronts at South Shields, Tynemouth, Cullercoats and Whitley Bay to catch a glimpse of her on her way to the breakers, her masts shortened to allow her to pass under the Forth Bridge. But the crowds were surprised and thrilled when she came to a halt about two miles off the Tyne piers.

Small boats crowded with sightseers went out to greet her. They sounded their sirens in tribute to the great liner. The 'flotilla' of craft was augmented by fishing vessels, tugs and the Shields pilot boat. It was a sad but heart-warming occasion.

Flying from *Mauretania*'s foremast was a 20ft-long blue ribbon, representing the Blue Riband of the Atlantic. Proudly, it bore the message: '1907 to 1929'.

The Lord Mayor of Newcastle, Councillor R.S. Dalgliesh, was at the North Shields ferry landing preparing to journey out to the ship when he received the following radio message from her:

'Thank you for your greeting. For twenty-eight years I have striven to be a credit to you, and now my day is done. Though I pass on, may Tyneside ever reach out to further and greater triumphs. With pride and affection I greet you. Farewell – Mauretania.'

The Lord Mayor and his party were then taken out to the ship by the tug *Plover*. The Mayor of South Shields, Councillor J.W. Watson, also made the journey, but in a separate boat. The councillors boarded the liner and chatted for several minutes to her last commander, Captain. A.T. Brown, on the bridge. Then it was time to leave. They re-boarded the *Plover*, the tug which had helped to bring *Mauretania* into and out of the river during her 1922 oil conversion. The party sang *Auld Lang Syne* as they stood in the tug. Many others in the host of small craft around them joined in the singing and then people aboard the liner also began to sing. There must have been tears in many eyes.

Soon *Mauretania* was steaming slowly away from the Tyne on the final leg of her final voyage. Boats again sounded their sirens and onlookers waved handkerchiefs until she was out of sight to the north. She was gone.

The Second Mauretania

A second ship named *Mauretania* was launched for Cunard in 1938 and completed the following year. However, she was not built on Tyneside. Instead, the order for the ship went to Cammell Laird of Birkenhead on the Mersey.

This beautiful 35,700-ton passenger liner bore two imposing funnels. During the Second World War the second *Mauretania* served as a hard-working troopship in the Indian and North Atlantic oceans. She returned to normal service after the war and during her last years, rather like her Tyne-built predecessor, she did spells of cruising. In 1965 she went to a breaker's yard on the shores of the Firth of Forth, exactly as the first *Mauretania* had done 30 years previously.

Compassion on the Sea

On the morning of April 15 1912 the Tyne-built passenger liner *Carpathia* rescued the bitterly cold and traumatised survivors of the *Titanic* disaster. She had been 58 miles away from the sinking ship when she picked up her distress call and she immediately responded by steaming into the night at full speed towards the *Titanic*'s reported position.

Carpathia braved numerous icebergs in the hope of reaching the stricken ship before she slipped beneath the surface of the North Atlantic. However, when she arrived at the disaster scene there was no sign of the great White Star liner which many had thought unsinkable. The *Titanic* had disappeared into the depths well over an hour previously with loss of more than 1,500 lives.

But *Carpathia* picked up the 705 *Titanic* passengers and crew who had managed to board the ship's lifeboats. To the survivors she must have seemed like a miracle as she steamed out of the dawn. *Carpathia*'s signal rockets had sparkled fitfully in the moonless night and then, as she drew closer, her porthole and mast lights had shone out like beacons of hope amid the gathering light. She was indeed a ship of hope, a liner of mercy bringing warmth and humanity out of a cruelly cold dawn.

Carpathia's birth on the River Tyne had been accompanied, like so many births, by emotions of pride and happiness. It was on April 24 1903 that the passenger cargo liner departed her fitting out quay at the Wallsend Shipyard of C.S. Swan and Hunter Ltd, which was soon to merge with Wigham Richardson's company at the Neptune Yard, Low Walker. Proud yard workers who had built her stood on the quay and cheered loudly as she began moving slowly down the Tyne for preliminary trials in the North Sea and delivery to her owners, Cunard, in Liverpool.

It was a thrilling moment for them to see the finished result of their labours and craftsmanship – she was yet another ship proving to the world the high standards achieved by the Tyne's naval architects and workmen.

Carpathia's keel had been laid down at Wallsend on September 10 1901 and she was launched just under a year later, on 6 August 1902. During the early stages of building the liner excavations in the yard had uncovered the eastern end of Hadrian's Wall, the so-called 'Branch Wall' leading down towards the river's edge from the Segedunum Roman Fort.

The 558ft-long vessel, bearing one tall funnel painted in Cunard's red and black livery, was 13,555 gross tons, making her one of the company's intermediate-sized liners. She was equipped with two quadruple expansion engines built by the Wallsend Slipway and Engineering Company, whose works were situated only a short distance down river from the shipyard. The engines were linked to two propellers which gave her a top speed of around 15 knots.

Carpathia was not a sumptuous luxury liner – she was built to carry second- and third-class passengers. But the ship provided, for relatively cheap fares, a superior standard of accommodation for such travellers than previously offered.

At the date of her completion she could take over 200 passengers in second class and more than 1,500 in third. Nearly 500 third-class (steerage) passengers were provided with cabins, including two, four and six-berth. But the majority in steerage were accommodated in dormitory areas.

Besides passengers, the liner was equipped to carry chilled beef from the United States in refrigerated compartments. *Carpathia* had fourteen steam winches and eighteen cargo derricks to enable speedy loading and discharging of cargo. Among the most important items she carried were the mails to and from America, earning her the title Royal Mail Steamship (RMS) *Carpathia*.

After several successful trial runs over the measured mile, during which *Carpathia* exceeded the guaranteed speed, the ship prepared for her delivery voyage under the command of

TWAS, Swan Hunter Archive

Wallsend creation. Carpathia on the stocks at C.S. Swan and Hunter's Wallsend Shipyard, 1902.

Captain Barr. After departing the Tyne, she steamed northwards around Scotland to reach Liverpool, as the *Mauretania* was to do four and a half years later. *Carpathia* sailed on her maiden voyage from Liverpool bound for Boston on 5 May 1903.

It was in 1912 that *Carpathia* became famous. At this time she was serving on the Trieste-New York route, carrying mainly Hungarian and Italian emigrants to a new life in the United States. Calls were made at Fiume (now Rijeka in Croatia), Palermo, Naples, Genoa and Gibraltar. On her return trips from New York to Trieste she would also take comfortably-off US citizens on pleasure trips to the Mediterranean.

There is an unwritten code among seamen, whether they be enemies in war or rivals in peace – to go to the aid of other mariners in distress. Captain Arthur Rostron, then master of *Carpathia*, could not have

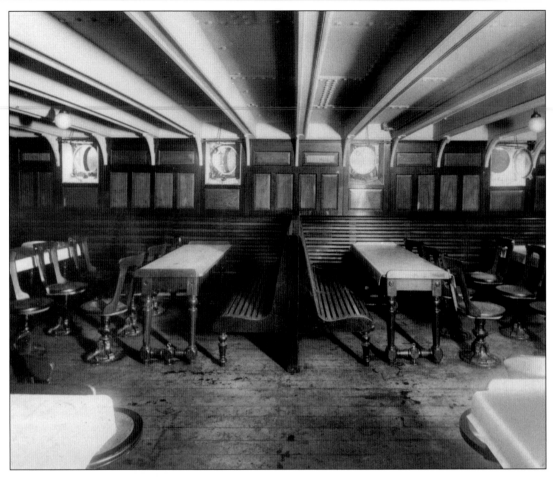

TWAS, Swan Hunter Archive

Very basic. Part of the third-class dining saloon. Carpathia carried many emigrants in third class from the Mediterranean to America.

been aware when his ship departed New York on April 11 1912 that he would soon be called upon to follow this law of the oceans in a humanitarian mission of epic proportions. As we have seen, he would later become the captain of *Mauretania*.

Rostron, who was born in Bolton, Lancashire, had been

an officer with Cunard since 1895 and was given command of *Carpathia* in January 1912 at the age of 42.

As his ship cleared New York harbour early on the afternoon of 11 April, another vessel on the other side of the Atlantic was departing from her anchorage off Queenstown while on her maiden voyage from Southampton to New York, a voyage she would never complete. This 46,300-ton liner, the biggest in the world at that date, was a four-funnel White Star giant carrying more than 2,200 passengers and crew. She bore a name destined to echo down the many years which have elapsed since. That one word – *Titanic* – remains indelibly printed on the face of 20th century history. Her maiden voyage was taking place amid a blaze of publicity with some people claiming that she was virtually unsinkable.

By the night of April 14 *Carpathia* was well on course for Gibraltar and about 1,000 miles east of New York. The weather had turned bitterly cold but the sky was wonderfully clear with many stars and the lights of the Aurora Borealis visible.

The ship's young wireless operator, Harold Cottam, had been on duty since the early morning. Only the biggest and most prestigious liners carried two operators in those early days of radio communication and so

TWAS, Swan Hunter Archive

An entrance lobby, showing a fine staircase. The ship's name can be seen on the floor covering.

Cottam had to work long hours. Throughout the day and evening he was busy relaying wireless messages (then known as Marconigrams) to and from passengers as well as other ships. He knew the *Titanic* was not far away. She was within the range of *Carpathia*'s wireless and Cottam heard her operators transmitting messages to the Cape Race station in

Newfoundland, Canada.

Another feature of his day had been a series of ice warnings from other ships. The first was from the Cunard passenger liner *Caronia* which reported sighting ice to the north of *Carpathia*. Later, reports of an icefield in the same area came from the White Star passenger liner *Baltic* and from the cargo steamers *Californian* and *Messaba*. These warnings were heard by *Titanic*.

The industrious Cottam passed the messages to the bridge and from them Rostron and his officers were able to calculate that *Carpathia* was well clear of the icefield to the north. Rostron surveyed the scene and could see no bergs or growlers (smaller blocks of ice) but the captain ordered that a sharp lookout be kept.

By just after midnight, Cottam was extremely tired and he began preparing to turn into bed for the night. However, the enthusiastic young operator kept his earphones on as he began unlacing his boots. Cottam called the *Titanic* to tell them there was a batch of messages on the airwaves for the ship. It was then that the *Titanic*'s radio operator butted in with an extraordinary message. He asked *Carpathia* to 'come at once' and added: 'We have struck an iceberg'. The operator gave *Titanic*'s position as Latitude 41.46 North, Longitude 50.14 West. He confirmed to Cottam they required immediate assistance.

Carpathia's stunned radio man raced from his wireless 'shack' to the bridge and told the officer on watch that *Titanic* had sent out a distress call. They then went to Rostron's cabin. The captain, who was trying to get some sleep, was irritated by their sudden entrance.

For a few seconds, he found the news that *Titanic* had hit a berg and was sinking difficult to believe. Could such a disaster really be happening to this great ship on her maiden voyage? He asked Cottam if he was absolutely certain the message was correct. The operator was adamant. *Titanic* had sent out the old distress call, CQD, and the new one, SOS.

The captain's doubts were ended. He went to the chart room where he worked out that the stricken liner's reported

TWAS, Swan Hunter Archive

Ready for her debut. Carpathia in dry dock at Liverpool before her maiden voyage in 1903. Note her two propellers and four masts. Equipped with 18 derricks, she carried refrigerated meat cargoes as well as passengers.

position was 58 miles to the north-west of *Carpathia*. Rostron sprang into immediate action. He ordered the ship to be turned around. *Carpathia* began moving on a north-westerly bearing as she worked up to full steam. She was now sailing in the opposite direction to Gibraltar, towards the ice-field.

Rostron showed efficiency and humanity as he meticulously prepared his ship for her rescue mission. Those members of the crew not on duty were roused from their sleep and the officers were assembled to be briefed by the captain on the tasks required.

He instructed that every member of the crew be served coffee to fortify them for the difficulties and hard work ahead. The measures taken were almost military in their thoroughness and attention to detail. The lifeboats were swung out in readiness to pick up survivors and canvas ash bags were brought out so that small children could be brought aboard in them if necessary. Bosun's chairs were also made ready to lift other survivors. Gangway doors were opened and lines prepared for throwing to *Titanic*'s lifeboats.

Ladders were fastened to *Carpathia*'s sides and strong lights sited at the gangways. Rostron told the stewards to have blankets, soup, tea, coffee and brandy ready. The two dining saloons became first aid stations and the ship's three doctors (British, Hungarian and Italian) were posted to them.

Captain Rostron was determined that *Carpathia* would be in a high state of readiness by the time she reached the disaster area. But could she reach the *Titanic* before she sank? The question must have plagued him continually as his ship raced through the early hours on a glass-like sea.

The captain did what he could to ensure the vessel's engines achieved their maximum potential. Her hot water was shut off so that all available heat could be turned into steam and extra stokers were employed keeping the furnaces fed. It is likely *Carpathia* achieved a speed of between 15 and 16 knots during the next few hours. Later, it would be claimed she had reached 17 knots or more, but this would not have been possible for her engines. However, it is beyond doubt that her Wallsend-built engines served her well.

Whatever her speed, Rostron must have been acutely aware of the risks ahead as he began the dash to the north-west in search of the ill-fated *Titanic*. His ship was carrying more than 700 passengers and she was sailing at full steam during the night into waters where an icefield had been reported. It was a dangerous situation and great care had to be taken with the helm. The lives of *Carpathia*'s passengers and crew as well as *Titanic*'s survivors were at stake.

Accordingly, extra seamen were posted to keep lookout and it was not long before the need for such action was confirmed. *Carpathia* began encountering a series of bergs and altered course to avoid them. A sharp lookout by officers and men proved effective and on at least one occasion a berg was spotted by star-shine reflected from its surface. *Carpathia* was, of course, a more easily manoeuvred ship than the much larger *Titanic* and was not travelling as fast.

Meanwhile, Cottam had radioed to *Titanic* that *Carpathia* was coming to their rescue as fast as she could.

At 2.40am a green flare was sighted from the bridge. It was a long way ahead but it sent a signal to *Carpathia* that human life was still active in the area of *Titanic*'s last reported position. In reply, at 3am *Carpathia* began firing rockets at 15-minute intervals. These would tell of the rescue ship's approach, giving hope to any survivors.

Rescue at Dawn

The ship continued to weave her way through the ice-field, with the eyes of lookouts strained towards the horizon. But as they approached the disaster area there was no sign of *Titanic*, though more green flares were sighted. Rostron must have known then that he was too late.

By 3.30am *Carpathia* found herself in the midst of countless bergs and growlers and Rostron ordered the engines to be put on half speed ahead. By about 4am the ship reached *Titanic*'s position and speed had been reduced to slow. They had taken around three-and-a-half hours to get there.

Suddenly, a green flare shone out. It was almost at sea level. Then, as the first light of dawn streamed across the water, Rostron and his men could just make out a lifeboat being rowed with difficulty towards *Carpathia*. All its occupants were exhausted, cold and numbed by their ordeal.

The boat contained 25 women, ten children and five men. Four of the men were at the oars, rowing in a way which betrayed their fatigue. At the tiller was a young ship's officer.

As the boat reached *Carpathia*'s side, an officer and two seamen descended rope ladders and boarded her. She was then manoeuvred towards an open doorway and made fast with lines. The women and children were lifted aboard safely in bosun's chairs and canvas ash bags. The five men managed to climb the ladder to the doorway.

As the light grew, Rostron was able to make out other lifeboats scattered over a wide area. There were 20 in all,

including four collapsibles. All around them were bergs and growlers which floated like white ghosts on the sea, although more solid than any phantom.

The young *Titanic* officer in the first boat, James Boxhall, was taken to the bridge where he told Rostron that the *Titanic* had sunk. The great liner had foundered at 2.20am on April 15 1912 with the loss of over 1,500 lives. It must have been difficult for Rostron and his crew to take in. The water in *Carpathia*'s vicinity was 33F, a mere one degree above freezing point. Anyone in the sea would not have lasted long. *Carpathia*'s crew continued the task of picking up the survivors. Her own passengers crowded the deck rails, watching the proceedings in stunned silence. Strangely, some of the boats were half empty, but others were packed to capacity with frightened souls chilled as much by their terrible ordeal as by a cold night on the Atlantic.

A great number of women survivors were now widows. They searched in vain for their husbands aboard the rescue ship. Children were also without fathers. Out of eleven honeymoon couples on *Titanic*, only one man survived. One woman had become separated from her baby during the evacuation of the *Titanic* but, unknown to her, the child had safely been taken aboard the rescue ship and happily Rostron was able to reunite mother and infant.

The last of the lifeboats to reach *Carpathia*'s side was carrying 75 people. It was very low in the water and in dan-

Courtesy of National Museums Liverpool (Merseyside Maritime Museum)

Disaster ship. The Titanic, which sank at 2.20 am on 15 April 1912. This photograph shows her leaving Southampton on 10 April. She called at Cherbourg and Queenstown before setting out on her passage to tragedy. Compare her vast size to that of Carpathia pictured on page 31.

ger of being swamped or capsized. The sea was becoming choppy. However, all were embarked safely. The final person to board was *Titanic*'s Second Officer, Charles Lightoller, who had taken command of the lifeboat and whose seamanship proved invaluable in keeping it afloat.

In all there were just 705 survivors, although some accounts suggest there may have been five or six more. The figure may therefore have been 510 or 511. Three men died of shock and exposure soon after they were taken aboard.

As the last of these unlucky yet lucky people were being picked up at 8.30am, the cargo ship *Californian* steamed into view from the west. She had been lying stopped amid the ice during the night and her radio operator had missed the *Titanic*'s distress call because he had gone to bed. She had now heard the news on the airwaves and asked Rostron if she could be of any help.

Carpathia became a ship pervaded by a profound sense of loss. Her flags were lowered to half mast and a service in remembrance of the dead and of thanksgiving for those rescued was held in the first-class dining saloon.

The ship steamed slowly around the waters above *Titanic*'s final resting place. Rostron was checking to see if there were any more survivors. But none were seen. Small items of wreckage were visible on the surface, including deck chairs. *Titanic* now lay more than 13,000ft below the surface of the Atlantic. She had broken in two.

The captain decided to land the survivors at New York and shortly before 9am ordered his ship to steam away from the wreck site to the south-west. They encountered numerous icebergs in their path, some as high as 200ft but eventually reached clear water after three hours of manoeuvring. They then set course for New York.

Californian had been requested to remain at the disaster scene to check for any possible survivors clinging to wreckage, but the temperature of the water meant that Rostron's hopes must have been fading fast.

Carpathia stopped briefly and a funeral service was held for the three men who had died and for a fourth who had passed away in one of the collapsible lifeboats. Their bodies were committed to the deep. The rescue ship's crew and passengers showed great kindness to the survivors and many gave up their cabins for them. Women passengers distributed clothes to survivors, some of whom had evacuated the ship wearing their dressing gowns or light clothing. Those people who had been in the water but who had managed to reach the boats had their wet clothes taken to the ship's ovens for drying.

As *Carpathia* steamed towards the shores of America, radio operator Cottam was deluged with Marconigrams from relatives of *Titanic* passengers and from newspapers seeking the stories of survivors and details of the rescue.

Rostron ordered that no information be divulged to the press. They would get their stories soon enough, when *Carpathia* docked. But the captain instructed that a list of survivors be transmitted to the Cape Race radio station. This was sent via the White Star liner *Olympic*, sister ship of *Titanic*.

Cottam was helped in his tasks by *Titanic*'s junior radio operator, Harold Bride, who had been among the rescued. They also transmitted messages to relatives of the survivors, but it was a difficult task because the air waves were crowded with inquiries.

Among the first-class passengers who lost their lives was John Jacob Astor, millionaire hotel owner, who had been returning to America with his 19-year-old pregnant wife Madeleine after visiting Europe and Egypt. Madeleine was one of the widows picked up by *Carpathia*. Also among the wealthy men lost was Benjamin Guggenheim of the US mining business empire.

Isidor Straus, owner of Macy's Department Store in New York, and his wife Ida were two other rich Americans who failed to return from the tragic maiden voyage. Ida had decided to remain on board with her husband. They bravely faced the end together as the slope of the great ship's decks grew steeper.

However, a larger proportion of third-class passengers

TWAS, Swan Hunter Archive

Mercy ship. Carpathia served on the New York-Trieste, Liverpool-New York and Liverpool-Boston routes. When she picked up the Titanic's distress call she was on her way to the Mediterranean.

lost their lives than first-class. Only 24 per cent of those travelling in third class were rescued as against 63 per cent in first class. The crew's survival rate was 23 per cent, almost the same as that of the poorest passengers. Only 210 of them lived to tread the decks of *Carpathia* out of 898.

In all, 1,503 people lost their lives in an ocean tragedy which shocked the world. *Titanic*'s master, Captain Edward Smith, honourably went down with his ship. All the liner's engineers also perished, a fate they shared with the ship's band, who, it is well attested, kept on playing until the very last.

The North-East of England, where *Carpathia* had started her life, did not escape the losses. Among the crew members who died was Alfred King, described by the *Newcastle Journal* as 'a promising youth of Nile Street, Gateshead'. He had worked for ship equipment manufacturers Clarke Chapman of Gateshead, but had always wanted to go to sea. Alfred had been employed as a lift boy in first class. Engineer C.F.W. Sidgwick, from Sunderland, was also lost. He was on his way to a new job in Mexico and his wife had been due to follow him at a later date. They were newly married.

William T. Stead, a famous campaigning journalist and former editor of the *Northern Echo* at Darlington, was another person on the casualty list. He had been born in Northumberland in 1849.

Lightning punctuated the skies and heavy rain drenched

Carpathia's decks as she entered New York Harbour on the evening of April 18th 1912. At The Battery thousands thronged the shore to watch her amid the storm. Lightning forked menacingly over the great city's skyline.

Carpathia berthed at Pier 54, from where she had started out, at 9.30pm and the survivors were disembarked safely. *Titanic* radio operator Harold Bride was carried ashore exhausted, his feet crushed and frost-bitten. The epic rescue was over.

The career of Captain Arthur Rostron never looked back after that momentous night in 1912. A plaque bearing his portrait was put on show in New York's Hall of Fame and he was presented with a US Congressional Medal of Honour. Later, he was to receive the Freedom of the City of New York. Other honours followed, including the Gold Medal of the New York Life Saving Benevolent Association and the Insignia of the French Legion of Honour.

Between 1915 and 1926 Rostron commanded *Mauretania*, including her spell as a hospital ship. In 1928 he was knighted, later becoming Commodore of the Cunard Line. Like the rockets he fired from his ship, he had shot to fame in one night of decisive action to save lives. But unlike the lights from those rockets, his fame never faded. The compassionate and efficient captain died in 1940.

And what became of *Carpathia*, the Wallsend-built rescue ship which was perhaps more famous than her captain? She continued on the Mediterranean run until 1915 when she was transferred to the New York-Liverpool route to carry vital supplies for Britain's war effort.

It was a German U-boat which eventually ended her career, ironically sending her to rest on the Atlantic seabed like the *Titanic*. *Carpathia* was steaming in convoy from Liverpool to New York on 17 July 1918. The ships were about 120 miles south west of the Fastnet Rock off the coast of southern Ireland and 170 miles north west of the Bishop Rock off Land's End, Cornwall. It was early morning. A U-boat began shadowing them. Its captain studied the convoy – there were three lines of ships. In the centre of the middle column a passenger-cargo liner stood out above the rest. She was *Carpathia*, the largest ship of all and an irresistible target to the commander of *U55*.

It was 9.15am. Two torpedoes hit the engine room amidships and another struck the vessel's forward section. Three trimmers and two firemen were killed by the first torpedo explosion. The attack also proved fatal to *Carpathia*. Captain William Prothero knew his ship would eventually sink, her injuries were too great, and he ordered everyone to take to the lifeboats. She slipped beneath the waves two-and-a-half hours later. The 275 survivors were picked up by the minesweeping sloop HMS *Snowdrop* which landed them safely at Liverpool.

The story of *Carpathia* had ended with a wartime attack, a fate she shared with many other merchant vessels of the First World War. But the liner from the Tyne had won for herself a lasting place in the honours list of humane deeds by ships and men.

By courtesy of the University of Liverpool Library D42/PR2/1/48/G2

Helping hands. Carpathia stewards, stewardesses, kitchen staff and other crew members pose for a picture in the aftermath of the rescue. Blankets, tea, coffee, soup and clothing were provided for survivors. Brandy was also available. Many passengers gave up their berths to Titanic's people.

The Spanish Beauty

One of the finest early passenger liners built on the Tyne was from Wigham Richardson's Neptune Yard, Low Walker, Newcastle. She was the Spanish vessel *Alfonso XII*, completed in 1888. *Alfonso XII* was launched by the twin daughters of the ship's captain. She had four raked (backwards sloping) masts and two funnels and also featured a clipper-style bow. The ship was designed mainly for service between Spain and Cuba.

Wigham Richardson's Neptune Yard was so proud of its new liner that after completion she was moved down river to Jarrow Slake where she was opened for public viewing. Tickets to see her cost one shilling each and the money raised was given to Whitley Bay Convalescent Homes.

However, *Alfonso XII*'s career was ended after barely 10 years of service. She was lost during the Spanish-American War of 1898 when she was hit by gunfire from American warships and ran aground on a reef off Port Mariel, Cuba.

In the 20th century, the Neptune Yard built the 15,700-ton French liner *Provence*. She was completed in 1951 and was constructed for a passenger service to South America, sailing from her home port of Marseilles. In 1954 *Provence* was involved in a collision in the River Plate with a tanker. Extensively damaged, she made it back to her home port for repairs.

Another liner born at Neptune was the 19,393-ton *Principe Perfeito* (Perfect Prince). *Principe Perfeito* was launched in September 1960 for Portuguese owners and served on the run between Lisbon and Mozambique.

TWAS, Swan Hunter Archive

Clipper-style bow. Alfonso XII was launched in 1888 by the twin daughters of the ship's captain.

Taking shape. Alfonso XII on the stocks at the Neptune Yard, Low Walker, Newcastle. She was completed in 1888. Safety precautions for the men were virtually non-existent.

TWAS, Swan Hunter Archive

A Trio of Monarchs

Three passenger liners featuring the name '*Monarch*' were built on the Tyne . It is easy to get them mixed up when recalling their history. However, although their names were similar each ship had a very different career.

The first of these ocean queens to set sail from the river was *Monarch of Bermuda*, launched on 17 March 1931 for the British company Furness Withy's New York-Bermuda cruise service. She was built at Vickers-Armstrongs' Walker Naval Yard in the east end of Newcastle. The order provided much needed work for the yard which had been forced to close in 1928 due to a lack of orders. To the delight of the workforce, it reopened again in 1930 to start the job of building this impressive three-funnelled ship.

The launch ceremony was performed by Lady Lewis, wife of Sir Frederick Lewis, chairman of Furness Withy and its associated companies. Hundreds of cheering workmen gathered to watch the event and crowds flocked to both sides of the river. Evidently all went smoothly.

Monarch of Bermuda was one of the first purpose-built cruise liners. The majestic vessel was 579 ft long and featured turbo-electric engines linked to four propellers, giving her a service speed of around 19.5 knots. Her gross tonnage was 22,400 and she could carry more than 800 passengers, most of them in first-class accommodation. The ship's three funnels, one of which was a dummy, gave her an elegant profile. *Monarch of Bermuda* ran her trials in the North Sea in

November 1931 and was completed later the same month. Sadly, the Walker Naval Yard then closed again because of the Depression which was gripping Europe and America. Tyne workmen who had created this ship were thrown on to the dole queue. Commander C.W. Craven, managing director of the Northern works and yards of Vickers-Armstrongs, had told the launch guests: 'My own company literally has not a single inquiry for any type of merchant vessel and I believe this is the state of affairs with practically all our competitors.'

The liner sailed on her maiden voyage from Southampton to New York in December 1931. Cruising between New York and Bermuda, she catered for rich Americans and Europeans, and two years later was joined by a sister ship, *Queen of Bermuda*. Her sister had been built in another part of the North, but was also the product of Vickers-Armstrongs. The *Queen* was launched at the company's Barrow-in-Furness yard in Cumbria. The two liners were appropriately dubbed the 'millionaires' ships'. Luxury cruising was their business.

It was while on one of these pleasure voyages in 1934 that *Monarch of Bermuda* was to encounter high drama and achieve what was perhaps her proudest moment. In the early hours of 8 September of that year a blaze broke out aboard the 11,500-ton American liner, *Morro Castle*, which was on a voyage from Havana to New York carrying tourists home from Cuba.

Going, gone! Hats off for the launch of Monarch of Bermuda as she leaves the slipway at the Walker Naval Yard on 17 March, 1931.

Mysteriously, the fire began in a writing room locker, but quickly spread through the ship's superstructure and was fanned by strong north-easterly winds. There was panic and confusion among the passengers.

The ship's captain had died suddenly, possibly of a heart attack, only a few hours before the blaze started and the first officer had taken over command. After an unsuccessful attempt by the crew to bring the blaze under control the new captain ordered an SOS message to be sent out by radio.

As the inferno raged a large liner with three funnels appeared out of the mist. She was the *Monarch of Bermuda*. The liner had been 30 miles away when she picked up *Morro Castle*'s distress call. Now the *Monarch* from the Tyne was steaming to the rescue with all the speed she could muster.

Other vessels were also converging upon the stricken ship's position, only six or seven miles off the New Jersey coast of America.

In driving rain and heavy seas the *Monarch*'s captain skilfully manoeuvred his ship to within less than 100ft of the *Morro Castle*'s side, creating an area of relatively sheltered water between the two vessels.

The Newcastle-built liner then launched two lifeboats which came alongside the flame-torn ship. The *Monarch*'s crew rescued 71 survivors. It was an operation carried out in the best traditions of humanitarian seamanship.

Other vessels also saved passengers from the blazing ship, but 137 lives were lost out of a total of 547 aboard. *Morro Castle* drifted ashore at Asbury Park, New Jersey, where

Majestic monarch. Monarch of Bermuda moves away from her fitting out quay at Wallsend in late 1931.

thousands flocked to watch the grim spectacle. With the outbreak of the Second World War in 1939 *Monarch of Bermuda* sailed back to the land of her birth and was refitted as a troopship. Painted grey, she was to carry soldiers to the Norwegian, Italian and North African campaigns. In 1940 the liner helped to evacuate troops from the Narvik area of Norway.

Surviving the war, *Monarch of Bermuda*'s career was nearly ended by disaster in 1947. While undergoing a refit in the Palmers dry dock at Hebburn in March that year she was badly damaged by fire. The blaze left her a virtual wreck and she was towed from the Tyne to the Firth of Forth and laid up. Her future did not look rosy. It seems that she came close to being scrapped. But fate was to prove kinder to the vessel. The Ministry of Transport purchased the ship and she underwent major repairs and extensive reconstruction at Southampton. A new liner was to emerge from the ashes of the old.

This time she was, rather sadly, equipped with only one funnel. Gone were the days of the three impressive raked (sloping) stacks. However, a special mast-like structure behind the bridge was also used for discharge of smoke. The ship's passenger accommodation was expanded to a capacity of over 1,590.

In the summer of 1950 *Monarch of Bermuda* embarked on a new chapter in her career. She became an emigrant ship on the run to Sydney, Australia, and was aptly renamed *New Australia*. The vessel was managed by the Shaw Savill & Albion Line on behalf of the Ministry of the Transport.

For over seven years the ship took hopeful Britons to a new life Down Under. But by 1958 many people were emigrating by air rather than sea and *New Australia* was sold to the Greek Line. Her name was changed again – this time to *Arkadia*. She was given an extensive refit and her length was increased by 11 ft. In May 1958, *Arkadia* was placed on the Bremerhaven-Canada route. She also sometimes sailed to her old stomping ground of Bermuda, as well as the Canaries and Bahamas.

The veteran Tyne-built liner went to the breaker's yard in Valencia, Spain, in December 1966. Her 35-year career was over but *Monarch of Bermuda* had proved herself a highly successful ship.

The second 'Monarch' from the Tyne's slipways was *Dominion Monarch*, launched at the Wallsend Shipyard of Swan Hunter & Wigham Richardson in July 1938 and completed in January the following year. She was built for Shaw Savill & Albion Line's service between Britain and New Zealand and at the time of her completion featured the most powerful diesel engines of any similar liner in the world. In addition, she was the third largest liner to be built on the Tyne, having a gross tonnage of 27,155.

The launch ceremony was performed by Lady Essendon on July 27 1938. She was the wife of the chairman of Shaw Savill & Albion, which by this time had been acquired by Furness Withy. Lord Essendon was also Furness Withy chairman. Guests cheered as well as thousands of spectators who had gathered on both sides of the river. The ship, which had been constructed on the same berth as *Mauretania*, was floating on the waters of the Tyne less than a minute after Lady Essendon broke the bottle of champagne against the vessel's bow.

Among those present were the High Commissioners of New Zealand, South Africa and Southern Rhodesia (now Zimbabwe) along with officials representing Australia. Also witnessing the launch were the Lord Mayor of Newcastle, Councillor G. Oliver, and the Lady Mayoress, and the Mayor and Mayoress of Wallsend, Alderman and Mrs James Paton.

The *Shipyard* magazine declared: 'Extensive welding is being carried out to the main members of the structure, comprising the butts and seams of plating of all decks, tank tops, bulkheads, casing, etc., whilst all weather decks will be sheathed with Burma teak.' Welding was then relatively new, but teak decks were a traditional, much-favoured material.

As well as carrying 524 passengers in single-class accommodation of first-class standard, the 682ft-long *Dominion Monarch* had a large cargo-carrying capacity. She was equipped with derricks, electric winches and six large cargo holds. The vessel could carry a total of 16,400 tons of cargo – most of it refrigerated food, including meat and dairy produce from New Zealand. She was the largest passenger-cargo liner of her type ever built. The ship provided work for the Wallsend Yard for about 18 months. Following the fitting out, Swan Hunter & Wigham Richardson directors gave permission for the men who had lovingly created her to take their wives on a tour around the liner, and large numbers took advantage of the opportunity.

In early January 1939 *Dominion Monarch* was drydocked at Palmers Hebburn yard in preparation for her trials in the North Sea. She was said to be the largest merchant vessel ever dry-docked on the Tyne at this date. The 700ft-long dock at Hebburn was by then owned by Vickers-Armstrongs following the collapse of Palmers.

Later in the month, *Dominion Monarch* left the river in rain and fog, escorted by four tugs, for her trials. She was towed stern first initially and then swung around to face the sea off Tyne Dock. The ship went on to notch up a speed of

Getting it right. Foremen adjust the champagne bottle prior to the launch of Dominion Monarch, July 1938.

21.5 knots on the trials off St Abb's Head, north of Berwick, and in service achieved an average of around 19.5 knots.

The liner sailed on her maiden voyage from London and Southampton to New Zealand in February 1939. For the outward passage, cargo was normally loaded in London and passengers were embarked at Southampton. Regular calls were made at Tenerife, Cape Town, Durban, Fremantle, Melbourne, Sydney and Auckland, with a turn-around at Wellington. The voyage to New Zealand took 35 days.

The ship gained a well-deserved reputation among travellers for being spacious and comfortable. Passenger facilities included a swimming pool, gymnasium and children's playroom. Safety features included 14 steel lifeboats, two motorboats and a sprinkler system in passenger areas in case of fire.

TWAS, Swan Hunter Archive

TWAS, Swan Hunter Archive

A ship is born. Dominion Monarch is launched at the Wallsend Shipyard on 27 July 1938.

Dominion Monarch's career was interrupted after only seven months of peacetime service by the outbreak of the Second World War in September 1939. During the conflict she served as a troopship, taking servicemen to and from such far-flung places as Egypt, Australia, New Zealand, the United States, the Middle East and India. She also carried much needed food supplies to Britain. Those six large cargo holds proved a great asset.

It was in December 1941 that the ship had a narrow escape. She was lying helpless in a Singapore dry dock as Japanese forces advanced down the Malayan Peninsula.

Singapore was soon to be invaded and it looked as if the Wallsend-built vessel would fall into the hands of the enemy. Her engines had been stripped down for repairs, but it turned out to be a race against time. The engineering crew worked unrelentingly to restore the liner's power and only a few weeks before the invasion she sailed out of Singapore harbour. It is said that the engineers were still putting the final touches to the repairs as the ship moved away.

Dominion Monarch was the last major vessel to escape safely from the harbour before its fall to the Japanese. The liner eluded attack and managed to reach New Zealand without mishap.

TWAS, Swan Hunter Archive

Testing time. Dominion Monarch leaves the Tyne for her trials.

In 1947, the ship was returned by the government to Shaw Savill & Albion. *Dominion Monarch* returned to the Tyne where the Swan Hunter workforce gave her a major refit lasting over a year. In December 1948 she resumed service on the Southampton-Wellington route and remained a popular liner throughout the 1950s. Her career ended in 1962 with an unusual duty. She was sold to a Japanese company who chartered her out to serve as a hotel ship during the World Fair at Seattle in the United States.

Dominion Monarch was soon, however, to sail for the breaker's yard. Ironically, after the Singapore escape, she was scrapped in Japan at the end of 1962 after a useful life during which she had proved herself to be an excellent example of Tyne workmanship.

The third '*Monarch*' to be delivered from the river was smaller, but perhaps more beautiful than her predecessors. She was *Ocean Monarch*, launched at Vickers-Armstrongs' Walker Naval Yard on July 27 1950. The ceremony was performed by the second Lady Essendon, whose father-in-law had been chairman of Furness Withy.

The liner was built as a replacement for *Monarch of Bermuda* on Furness Withy's New York-Bermuda cruise service. The 13,650-ton *Ocean Monarch* was to return to Walker for refits. She was much smaller than her predecessor and had only one funnel – but she was elegant, stylish and looked not unlike a royal yacht.

The ship was designed to appeal to the largely American travellers who were her main customers. Indeed, the *Newcastle Journal* declared the vessel to be 'a dollar seeker'.

The interior was furnished with inch-deep carpets and timbered stairways. The dining saloon extended the full width of the ship and was lined with mirrors and

TWAS, *Turners*

In her element. Ocean Monarch shortly after her launch at the Walker Naval Yard, Newcastle in 1950.

coloured frescoes depicting birds, mammals and fish. Passengers were served cocktails from a bar counter of golden onyx marble. Although she was small, there was clearly little lacking in luxury.

Facilities for the 440 single-class passengers included a cinema with seating for 140, a beauty parlour, a swimming pool with floodlighting and elevators between decks.

Perhaps the crowning glory of the ship was a figurehead on the prow which appropriately depicted the ocean monarch, King Neptune. A second effigy of the mythical ruler of the deep, flanked by sea horses, adorned a bulkhead on the promenade deck.

Ocean Monarch ran preliminary trials off the Tyne in late March 1951, followed by official trials on the measured mile in the Firth of Clyde, during which she clocked up a speed of 20 knots.

The new liner sailed on her maiden voyage to New York in April 1951. She was used mainly on cruises to Bermuda and the West Indies, but voyages were also arranged to the St Lawrence River in Canada and nearby waters.

For 15 years *Ocean Monarch* enjoyed a successful career with the Furness Bermuda Line, a subsidiary of the Furness Withy company. Her career was not without incident. The liner answered a distress call from the Dutch tanker *Astrid Naess*, which was hit by fire off the coast of Virginia. Seven men with burns, two of them serious, were transferred to the Tyne ship which was the nearest vessel carrying a doctor. The injured were then taken safely to New York.

In 1967 Furness Withy sold *Ocean Monarch* to a Bulgarian state tourist company. The ship was renamed *Varna* and steamed off on cruises from the Black Sea to visit such ports as Istanbul, Athens and Alexandria. This time, of

TWAS, Turners

Graceful lady. Ocean Monarch, completed in 1951.

course, her passengers were Bulgarians of moderate income rather than affluent Americans.

The year 1978 saw the liner change hands again. *Varna* was bought by Dolphin (Hellas) Shipping, of Greece, who eventually renamed her *Reina del Mar*. The company planned to give her a refit and use her for Mediterranean cruising. But it was not to be. Fate intervened to abruptly cut short her career.

As work began on refitting the newly-named *Reina del Mar* close to the Greek port of Piraeus in 1981 a fire broke out in the depths of the vessel which spread to the passenger areas. Although no-one appears to have been hurt, the former *Ocean Monarch* was engulfed by the flames, capsized and became a total loss. All three of the Tyne's 'Monarchs' were now gone.

The Castle of Safety

In 1925 Vickers-Armstrongs' Walker Naval Yard, Newcastle, completed the passenger liner *Gripsholm* for the Swedish America Line's Gothenburg-New York service. She was also used for cruising.

The 574ft-long vessel was the first passenger liner on the North Atlantic to be driven by diesel engines. During the Second World War the two-funnel *Gripsholm* served as an International Red Cross ship. Her duties included transporting diplomats, exchanging prisoners of war, and repatriating people, including the wounded. The ship had been named after a famed red-brick castle in Sweden, and in her wartime role she became a peace-loving 'castle' of safety

Swedish queen. Gripsholm moves into dry dock at Hebburn in 1925.

for her passengers. She bore red crosses on her hull and funnels.

In 1949 *Gripsholm* underwent extensive reconstruction. The vessel was lengthened, her gross tonnage increased from around 17,400 to 19,100, the passenger accommodation was revamped and she was given two new funnels. In 1954 the ship was transferred to the German flag, and sailed on voyages to New York for the Bremen-Atlantic Line. The following year she was renamed *Berlin*. The former *Gripsholm* went to the breaker's yard in late 1966.

The Pride of Norway

The Norwegian liner *Bergensfjord* was the pride of her country's merchant fleet and a fine example of Tyne shipbuilding skills. She was built at Swan Hunter & Wigham Richardson's Wallsend Yard for the Norwegian America Line, being completed in May 1956 – a month ahead of the scheduled contract date.

Bergensfjord's keel was laid down at Wallsend in June 1954. The liner was launched in July 1955 by Princess Astrid of Norway. A guard of honour was provided for the princess by cadets from the Norwegian sail training ship *Sorlandet*. Over 5,000 people watched the event.

The 18,700-ton vessel was 578ft long and was equipped with stabilisers and an all-welded aluminium superstructure. The aluminium in the ship was probably the most extensive use of the material in any vessel at that date. Its lightness led to a great saving in weight, which meant that additional passengers could be carried. The aluminium also enabled greater space to be given to lounges, bars, dining areas and other public rooms and more clear space generally for passengers. Combined with its durable qualities, the material was considered an excellent choice.

The one-funnel, twin-propeller motor ship was designed for a normal service speed of 20 knots on the Oslo-Copenhagen-New York route. This was a summer-only service by the mid-1950s and the vessel was employed in cruising at other times.

Bergensfjord carried 125 first-class passengers, 730 tourist class, and 351 crew. The large number of tourist class passengers reflected the company's view that the majority of people wished to travel in comfort but not necessarily in luxury.

But the word comfort belied the fact that *Bergensfjord* was nevertheless a liner with a stylish and beautiful interior with a distinctly Scandinavian touch. Decoration was in the modern Scandinavian style with extensive use being made of light colours, tapestries, paintings and large and small decorated glass walls.

The largest woven tapestry, in the first-class dining room, was 19ft long and depicted a scene from Norwegian history – the wedding in the 1290s of Duke Haakon, later King Haakon V, at Akershus Castle, Oslo. This was just one example of the major contribution Norwegian artists made to the interior.

In the first-class smoking rooms there were two 7ft-long paintings showing scenes from Bergen life, and a tourist-class hallway featured two mosaics depicting Norwegian historical scenes. In addition, the tourist class library and writing room contained paintings of the country's Telemark district, and the main ballroom had a beautiful, high, domed ceiling. One side of the room was fitted with a decorated glass screen.

The ship also featured two observation lounges, two swimming pools, one portable, a covered promenade deck with large windows, a children's playroom, a garden lounge complete with plants, a shopping centre, several bars and an impressive curved staircase with strip lighting below each tread. Outside the summer season, when the liner was used for cruising, the tourist and first-class areas were combined to form a one-class liner.

Bergensfjord left the Tyne in April 1956 for her trials which took place off the Scottish coast. Near Fair Isle, between Orkney and the Shetlands, she ran into a Force 8 gale and the ship began rolling 16 degrees. But as soon as the stabilisers were put into operation the rolling was greatly reduced.

From Fair Isle the liner journeyed southwards to the measured mile off St Abb's Head in Berwickshire, where her speed was tested. She achieved a top rate of nearly 24 knots and clocked up an average of 22.

Bergensfjord left the Wallsend Shipyard for delivery to the Norwegian America Line in May 1956. She was intended to be the flagship of the Norwegian merchant fleet and her arrival was eagerly awaited in Oslo.

TWAS, *Turners*

Princess Astrid of Norway on the platform for the launch of the Bergensfjord at Wallsend in July 1955.

On the 14th of the month the workers who had built the liner watched her slip gracefully away from the fitting-out quay and pass down the Tyne amid cheering and proud enthusiasm. When she reached the North Sea the Red Ensign was lowered and the Norwegian America Line house flag hoisted. On board were representatives of Swan Hunter. *Bergensfjord* was in good hands. Her captain for the North Sea crossing was the commodore of the line, Captain Olaf Bjornstad, who brought the liner *Stavangerfjord* safely home to Norway in 1953 after losing a rudder in an Atlantic storm.

After a calm crossing, the liner approached Bergen on May 15. As she drew nearer the Norwegian coastline the first signs of the tremendous welcome that awaited her became visible. Ships were dressed overall with flags and penants and small craft crowded with people eager to catch a glimpse of the vessel came out from the mainland to greet her.

As she sailed up the fjord towards Bergen, officials of Swan Hunter noticed another ship, close astern, following her. It was the 22-knot North Sea ferry *Leda*, which had been completed by Swan Hunter in 1953. *Leda* had been the first

TWAS, Turner's

Launched by a princess. Bergensfjord is launched, 18 July 1955, by Princess Astrid of Norway at Swan Hunter's Wallsend yard.

North Sea ferry to be equipped with stabilisers and had also been launched by Princess Astrid. The shipbuilding company officials watched with pride as the two Tyne ships glided together through the calm waters of the fjord and moored opposite each other at Bergen pier. At the time they were the fastest vessels in the Norwegian merchant service.

Bergensfjord then sailed on to Stavanger, Kristiansand and Oslo on a two-day cruise in which she received a warm and enthusiastic welcome from the Norwegian people.

Perhaps the greatest welcome was given to her when she reached Oslo on 17 May – Norwegian Independence Day. Despite the cold wind and rain, hundreds thronged the quay where the ship berthed. A band played, countless flags were unfurled and nearby vessels sounded their sirens. On 18 May the chairman of Swan Hunter, Mr J.W. Elliott, was made a Commander of the Royal Order of St Olav. On May 30 the ship left Oslo on her maiden voyage to New York.

After a successful career with the Norwegian America Line *Bergensfjord* was sold to the CGT Line of France in 1971, renamed *De Grasse* and used for cruising.

However, in 1974 she changed hands again and was bought by Thoresen and Company (Singapore) Ltd. The liner was used as a cruise ship in Malaysian waters and was based in Singapore. Her name was changed to *Rasa Sayang*.

In 1978 came another change of ownership, *Rasa Sayang* was sold to Sunlit Cruises, of Cyprus, and renamed *Golden Moon*. Then, in 1980, she was sold to a Greek shipowner, who planned to charter her out as a cruise ship operating from Australia. She was given back her old name of *Rasa Sayang* and sent for a refit. But while this work was taking place at the Greek port of Piraeus in late 1980, she was severely damaged by a blaze.

The ship was towed away from the shore towards Kynosoura, just outside Piraeus harbour, where she keeled over and sank, half submerged. Ironically, the wreck was to be joined by another, that of the Tyne-built *Ocean Monarch*, the following year. She came to rest close to the former *Bergensfjord*. As we have seen, *Ocean Monarch*, at that time bearing the name *Reina del Mar*, was also the victim of fire.

The career of *Bergensfjord* had ended sadly. She had been the pride of Norway. But the beautiful liner had served her purpose well by giving nearly 25 years of sound service and had ably demonstrated the skills of the Tyne in the fine art of shipbuilding.

Drama off the Tyne

During World War II the Norwegian America Line suffered heavy shipping losses. Among the vessels of the line sunk by enemy action was the two-funnel *Oslofjord*, which entered transatlantic service in 1938. However, in 1940 she was laid up at New York and requisitioned as a troopship by the British later that year.

In December 1940, while on a voyage from Liverpool to Newcastle to be fully fitted out for trooping, *Oslofjord* struck a German mine laid by an aircraft off the mouth of the Tyne. One crew member lost his life, but the others were saved, many being rescued by the Tynemouth and Cullercoats lifeboats.

The wreck now lies south of the pier at South Shields. *Oslofjord* suffered an additional indignity when in 1943 a cargo vessel, the *Eugenia Chandris*, sank on top of her.

A Cunard Quartet

In the years 1920-25 Tyne shipyards built four passenger liners for Cunard's Britain-Canada services. Each could carry around 1,700 passengers.

They were *Ascania* and *Ausonia*, from Vickers-Armstrongs' Walker Naval Yard, *Aurania*, from Swan Hunter & Wigham Richardson's Wallsend Yard, and *Andania*, from Hawthorn Leslie's Hebburn Yard. Most of these 'A-Class' vessels were in the region of 13,900 tons and they were driven by steam turbine engines linked to twin propellers. This gave each ship a speed of about 16 knots.

Cunard had suffered heavy losses of its Canadian ships during the First World War and the new liners were designed as replacements. During the Second World War, *Andania* was torpedoed and sunk by a U-boat 70 miles south east of Iceland in June 1940 while serving as an armed auxiliary cruiser. However, the ship took a considerable time to sink and all the crew were taken off safely. Two men were injured.

Cunard

Cunard R.M.S. "Ascania"

TWAS, Swan Hunter Archive

Lined up for the launch. Guests at the launch of the Aurania at Swan Hunter & Wigham Richardson's Wallsend Shipyard in February 1924.

The Empress

TWAS, Turners

The second largest liner to be built on the Tyne was *Empress of Canada*, built for Canadian Pacific's transatlantic service. The ship's gross tonnage (a measurement of cubic capacity within the vessel) was 27,280 and this made her second in size only to the legendary *Mauretania* of 1907. Swan Hunter's *Dominion Monarch* of 1939 came a close third.

The liner destined to ply between Britain and Canada was launched by Mrs Deifenbaker, wife of Canadian prime minister John Deifenbaker, at Vickers-Armstrongs' Walker Naval Yard, Newcastle, on May 10, 1960. She was completed in March the following year.

As *Empress of Canada* left the Tyne on her delivery voyage to Liverpool in 1961, escorted by five tugs, thousands of people lined the banks of the river to cheer her. Tynesiders have always enjoyed seeing their great ships depart the river. Other vessels sounded their sirens in salute to the largest post-war liner to be built for the Canadian Pacific fleet. The *Empress* answered her well-wishers by sounding her own, deep-voiced siren, saluting the proud workers who had lovingly brought her into life. The one-funnel liner, which was 650ft long and topped by a stack weighing 64 imperial

Bow view. Empress of Canada in dry dock, before her maiden voyage in 1961. Note the bulbous bow.

tons, was a majestic sight as she glided towards the North Sea. It is said 20,000 rivets were used in her construction – but the hull and other areas also featured extensive welding. She had provided work for around 2,000 Walker yard men.

The turbine engines of *Empress of Canada*, driving twin propellers, enabled her to achieve a service speed of 20 knots, although she had clocked up 23 knots on trials.

The ship could accommodate 192 first-class and 856 tourist-class passengers. Built for Canadian Pacific's Liverpool-Greenock-Quebec City-Montreal service, she also went cruising in the winter and would then carry 1,080 passengers in single-class cabins. The Caribbean and Mediterranean were favourite cruise destinations for the ship. She was the new Canadian Pacific flagship and was known to many people by her alternative name – the 'White Empress'.

Many of her cabins featured finely-crafted wood panelling as well as toilet and bath or shower facilities. Canadian Pacific also pointed out that passengers were able to adjust the temperatures in their fully air-conditioned accommodation – this was something of a novelty in the early 1960s.

The liner's bulbous bow was designed to reduce pitching and she was also equipped with stabilisers. On her maiden voyage the

TWAS, *Turners*

Grand debut. Crowds assemble for the launch of Empress of Canada in 1960.

Empress encountered a 60mph gale and 30ft head-on waves and was said to have ridden the storm 'magnificently'.

The ship remained on the Liverpool-Montreal route for 10 years. However, in November 1971 the decline in passenger numbers on the sea route to Canada forced her withdrawal and she was laid up at Tilbury with an uncertain future.

Luck proved to be on her side. In February 1972 a newly-formed American company, Carnival Cruise Lines of Miami, purchased the liner and placed her on Caribbean service. She was the company's first ship. The *Empress of Canada* was renamed *Mardi Gras*.

Her maiden cruise for the new company included a minor drama. As she left Miami in March 1972 *Mardi Gras* became stranded on a sand bar just outside the harbour entrance. The vessel had to be pulled off by tugs before she could resume her first leg of the voyage – to San Juan, Puerto Rico.

During her career with Carnival Cruise Lines she was also sometimes based at Fort Lauderdale in Florida and was sent on pleasure trips to Nassau and Freeport in the Bahamas. It seems the ship played an important role in reviving the popularity of cruising, which today is flourishing. *Mardi Gras* was well-liked by her mainly American passengers, and facilities aboard this floating holiday resort included two outdoor swimming pools, a children's paddling pool, an indoor pool, a casino, disco, cinema, health room and sauna, duty-free shops, a hairdresser's salon, exercise room, ballroom and hospital.

In 1993, after a little over 10 years with Carnival, the liner which had been born in the cool waters of the Tyne was acquired by the Greek company Epirotiki Line. Cruising continued to be her business and she was sometimes chartered out and bore a number of temporary names. These were *Olympic*, *Star of Texas* and *Lucky Star*. Eventually Epirotiki named her *Apollon* and she bore this for most of her remaining career.

In 1999 *Apollon* was chartered out to Britain's Direct Cruises, being given the temporary name of *Apollo* for this short spell of her life. The following year she returned to her Greek owners. By this time Epirotiki Line had been transformed into the Royal Olympic Line as the result of a merger. *Apollon* sailed out of Piraeus harbour in Greece on a few more relatively short cruises, but the end was near. In late 2003 the former *Empress of Canada* went to the breaker's yard. Her career had lasted 32 years.

TWAS, Turners

Empress of Canada.

Another Empress

Empress of Canada was not the first passenger liner to be built at Vickers-Armstrongs' Walker Naval Yard for Canadian Pacific. In 1957 the yard had completed the smaller 22,585-ton *Empress of England*.

This vessel had been launched the previous year by Lady Eden, wife of prime minister Sir Anthony Eden. *Empress of England* sailed on her maiden voyage from Liverpool to Montreal in April 1957.

She was sold to Shaw Savill & Albion in 1970 and placed on voyages to Australia, being somewhat confusingly renamed *Ocean Monarch*. The former *Empress of England* went to the breaker's yard in 1975 after a relatively short career.

Walker launch. Tugs attend to the Empress of England after her launch at Vickers-Armstrongs Walker Naval Yard, Newcastle, in 1956. The yard's large cranes are prominent in this picture taken from Bill Quay.

TWAS, Turners

Built for the India Run

As well as the great shipping companies of Canadian Pacific and Cunard, three passenger ships were built on the Tyne in the 1920s for Britain's famed P&0 Line, which served India, Australia and the Far East.

In 1923, the workforce of Armstrong Whitworth's Walker Naval Yard (later Vickers-Armstrongs) completed the P&0 liner *Mongolia*, of 16,385 tons, which operated on the Britain-India-Australia route during her early years. *Mongolia* went on to have a varied career lasting over 40 years.

In addition, Hawthorn Leslie's Hebburn Yard constructed the two-funnel *Ranpura* and *Ranchi* for P&0's Tilbury-Bombay service. These ships later did a spell on the run to China and Japan. *Ranpura* was launched in September 1924 and *Ranchi* early the following year. Their tonnage was around 16,585.

Hawthorn Leslie also launched two passenger liners of around 10,000 tons each for the British India Line. These two-funnel sisters were *Talma*, completed in 1923, and *Tilawa,* delivered the following year. They served on a route between Calcutta and Japan. *Tilawa* was sunk by a Japanese submarine in 1942.

Eastern queens. Top, a cabin on Ranpura. Below, Talma or Tilawa. All three ships were built at Hawthorn Leslie's Hebburn Yard.

TWAS, Swan Hunter Archive

TWAS, Swan Hunter Archive

Ranpura, built for P&O's run to India.

TWAS, Swan Hunter Archive

Seagoing Cities

During the years 1952-1954 the Walker Naval Yard constructed four handsome passenger-cargo liners for Ellerman Lines. They were *City of Port Elizabeth*, *City of Exeter*, *City of York* and the last to be delivered, *City of Durban*. Each ship had a tonnage of around 13,300 and each could carry just over 100 passengers as well as substantial amounts of cargo. Many cabins featured fine wood furniture and panelling.

The 'City' quartet served on the route between London and Beira in Mozambique. Their ports of call were Las Palmas, Cape Town, Port Elizabeth, East London, Durban and Lourenco Marques (now Maputo).

TWAS, Turners

Built for the Africa route. City of Durban, launched for Ellerman Lines at the Walker Naval Yard.

TWAS, Turners

The well-equipped nursery aboard City of Exeter.

TWAS, Turners

City of Exeter, another 'city' class ship from the Walker Naval Yard.

An Unlucky Star

The Tyne-built passenger liner *Northern Star*, measuring 24,000 tons, could be regarded as an unlucky ship. The description is perhaps a little unfair since many years of her career were trouble-free. However, from the start the ship had more than her fair share of problems and mishaps.

Northern Star was launched by the Queen Mother at Vickers-Armstrongs' Walker Naval Yard, Newcastle, in June 1961.

At that date the vessel was unusual in two major respects – her engines and 43ft-high funnel were positioned aft and she carried no cargo. This enabled the main body of the ship to be given over to passenger accommodation and facilities without the layout problems created by engines amidships and cargo holds.

The 20-knot vessel was essentially a floating hotel for a little over 1,400 passengers. She was built for Shaw Savill & Albion Line's round-the-world service, which she operated in tandem with her older and slighter smaller sister ship, *Southern Cross*, which carried just under 1,200 passengers.

Northern Star circumnavigated the globe in an eastwards direction, and her 20,000-ton sister, which had been completed in 1955, went the other way around. Her ports of call included Cape Town, Fremantle, Sydney and Wellington, returning home via Panama to Southampton. Stops were also made in the Canary Islands and Tahiti.

The misfortunes encountered by the liner began from the start of her career. During the launching ceremony at Walker an alarm bell rang when a fuse box overheated. It proved to be a portent of worse to come.

As the liner was about to leave the Tyne after completion in June 1962 she nearly met disaster. A gust of wind swept her suddenly around at right angles and she almost rammed the pier at South Shields.

For half an hour tugs fought to control the huge vessel. They were forced to swing her round stern first so that she left the river facing in the wrong direction. It was an undignified start to her career, but the liner had been saved from damage. The deck crew and tug skippers were praised for their alert efforts.

But trouble struck *Northern Star* again a month later on her maiden voyage around the world. The ship developed engine problems off the west coast of Africa and arrived in Cape Town a day late. In September she encountered more engine trouble on her homeward journey between Tahiti and Panama and was forced to travel at reduced speed.

But the bad luck which had dogged her was not yet over. In June 1963 the ship was in danger when gale force winds swung her twice against a wharf at Wellington, New Zealand.

The following month tragedy struck a member of the crew. The bosun's mate aboard the liner was accidentally killed at Port of Spain, Trinidad, when he fell through a side doorway as a gangway was being lowered. A rope he was carrying wrapped around his neck.

Mercifully, the next few years remained free of any major mishaps, but in November 1967 1,000 passengers had to be evacuated at Durban when fire broke out on board.

Northern Star finished the year on another unlucky note. In December, with 1,350 passengers aboard, she ran on to a reef during a storm at the entrance to Papeete harbour in Tahiti, but was eventually freed. This could have been disastrous.

There then followed six years of voyages with little or no problems. It seemed that the liner would finish her career in grand style. But it did not turn out that way.

In June 1974 boiler trouble developed on a cruise in the Mediterranean and she docked five days late at her home port of Southampton with only 100 of the original 1,000 passengers on board. The rest had been flown home.

Northern Star was withdrawn from service in the autumn of 1974 and after a life of only 14 years she undertook her last voyage – to the breaker's yard at Kaohsiung, Taiwan, in 1976. She had been the Tyne's unlucky star, but former yard workers still recall her proud name, so appropriate for a North-built ship, and her unusual looks.

Short career. Northern Star, completed at the Walker Naval Yard in 1962.

TWAS, Turners

Stylish Italian

In the autumn of 1921 Swan Hunter & Wigham Richardson completed the Italian passenger liner *Giulio Cesare* (Julius Caesar) for the Navigazione Generale Italiana of Genoa. The 21,600-ton ship was built at the Wallsend Yard. She sailed on her maiden voyage from Genoa via Naples to Buenos Aires in May 1922.

A particularly elegant ship, the two-funnel *Giulio Cesare* featured a first-class dining saloon reminiscent of *Mauretania*'s – there were two floors crowned by a single glass dome. She could carry 2,870 passengers and crew. A total of 244 passengers had luxury staterooms with bath and shower facilities. Some of these suites had a private sitting room and dining room attached. They featured oak parquet floors. Marble-topped washbasins were also provided and bathroom walls and floors were tiled.

TWAS, Swan Hunter Archive

On trials. Giulio Cesare, completed by Swan Hunter & Wigham Richardson at the Wallsend Shipyard in 1921. She is seen here on her trials.

Giulio Cesare's career was abruptly ended during the Second World War. In September 1944 she was badly damaged during an Allied air raid near Trieste on the Adriatic. The ship was hit by rockets fired by South African Beaufighter aircraft while she was at anchor. It was a sad fate for such a fine liner.

TWAS, Swan Hunter Archive

Splendid elegance. The beautiful first-class dining room of the Italian liner Giulio Cesare.

Rescued and Bombed

During the decade before the First World War, Swan Hunter & Wigham Richardson launched two superb-looking sister passenger liners for Cunard's Liverpool-Boston service. They were *Franconia* and *Laconia*, each having a gross tonnage of around 18,100 and each sporting two, tall funnels.

Franconia was launched in July 1910 and completed in early 1911. *Laconia* was launched in July 1911 and completed the following December. However, both ships were lost during the First World War within six months of each other. *Franconia* was torpedoed by a U-boat in October 1916 in the Mediterranean while serving as a troopship. In February 1917, *Laconia* also fell victim to a U-boat while in the North Atlantic.

A second *Laconia* was built on the Tyne after the First World War. She was also launched at Swan Hunter & Wigham Richardson's Wallsend Yard. The 19,680-ton vessel's career had an

TWAS, *Swan Hunter Archive*

Two-funnel beauty. The Franconia in Palmers' dry dock at Hebburn, early in 1911. She was sunk during World War I.

Hat parade. Top guests at the launch of the first Laconia on 27 July, 1911. Like her sister, Franconia, Laconia was sunk during World War I. On the extreme right, with bowler and white beard, is Swan Hunter & Wigham Richardson Chairman, George B. Hunter.

TWAS, Swan Hunter Archive

TWAS, Swan Hunter Archive

The gymnasium aboard Franconia.

inauspicious start in 1920 when the French passenger liner *Meduana*, which was being fitted out at Swan's, caught fire, keeled over in the river and blocked the end of *Laconia*'s slipway. This meant the launch had to be postponed. She was eventually launched in April 1921 after two more delays.

The second *Laconia* sailed on her maiden voyage to New York in May 1922. However, the ship encountered tragedy during the Second World War. In September 1942, while homeward bound from Egypt, she was torpedoed and sunk by a U-boat in the South Atlantic. *Laconia* was carrying Britons, Poles and Italian prisoners of war. Survivors, including women and children, took to the lifeboats.

Later, the commander of the U-boat which had attacked the ship decided to mount a rescue operation. The U-boat

TWAS, Swan Hunter Archive

The first Laconia on the stocks. She was built for Cunard's Liverpool-Boston service.

took the lifeboats in tow and a considerable number of survivors were transferred to the submarine, both on deck and below. Conditions became crowded. The U-boat commander then sent out a radio message calling on ships in the vicinity

TWAS, Swan Hunter Archive

The second Laconia is towed from the Tyne by a tug in 1922. She was torpedoed and sunk in 1942.

to steam to the rescue. Two other U-boats and an Italian submarine joined the rescue a few days later. They supplied food and water to the survivors.

However, events were to take a dramatic turn. An American Liberator aircraft dropped six bombs on the U-boat which had begun the rescue. The plane also dropped depth charges. As a result of the attack, one of the lifeboats capsized and the submarine was badly damaged. The U-boat had been displaying the Red Cross flag.

Eventually, the 1,111 survivors were picked up by the Vichy French cruiser *Gloire* and her escorting vessels who landed them safely at Cassablanca in Morocco. More than 2,000 people lost their lives as a result of the sinking. Afterwards, Germany's U-boats were ordered to stop the practice of picking up survivors from torpedoed ships. The controversial episode became known as the '*Laconia* Incident'.

The Last Queen

The last passenger liner constructed on the Tyne was *Vistafjord*, launched at Swan Hunter's Neptune Yard on 15 May 1972 for the Norwegian America Line. However, she was never intended to be a scheduled transatlantic route liner operating between Norway and New York on a regular basis. By the late 1960s the jet aircraft had well and truly taken over the passenger trade between Europe and North America. As early as 1958 the death-knell of the old-style Atlantic liners had been sounded. In that year, for the first time, more people travelled by air than by sea between Western Europe and the United States and Canada. *Vistafjord* was built to be part of a new generation of passenger ships – the cruise liners.

Surprisingly, the launch ceremony was a low-key occasion. There was no fashionable lady to perform the honours, nor any champagne to break against the ship's bows. *The Journal*, Newcastle, reported that Kaare Haugh, Norwegian America Line's technical director, and Tom McIver, deputy chairman of Swan Hunter, 'simply pulled the handle to start the triggers holding the ship back'.

Mr Haugh indicated there would be a celebration and champagne would flow when *Vistafjord* was delivered to Oslo and he hoped this would be in time for Norwegian Independence Day, 17 March, the following year.

He was not to be disappointed. The 629ft-long vessel was delivered to her owners in Oslo exactly a year after her

Fitting out. Vistafjord alongside her fitting out quay at the Neptune Yard in February 1973.

ncjMedia

Norway bound. Vistafjord passes fishing boats at North Shields as she leaves the Tyne on her delivery voyage to Norway in May 1973.

launch. This was several months ahead of the contract date. The ship was a true 'queen' of the Neptune Yard. On 22 May 1973 *Vistafjord* left Oslo on her maiden voyage to New York via Copenhagen.

The Norwegian America Line were obviously delighted with their latest and largest passenger ship. Fixtures and fittings had been brought from many countries to furnish the interior, including France, Italy, Denmark, Sweden, Norway, West Germany and Taiwan.

The chairman of the line, Leif Hoegh, described Swan Hunter as 'The top passenger ship builders of the world today.' *Vistafjord* did not neglect her North-East origins. In August 1975 she called in at the Tyne for the start of a cruise to the Baltic.

However, the magnificent vessel was to be the last passenger ship built for the Norwegian America Line. In 1980 the passenger cruise division of the company was purchased by Leif Hoegh & Co. Included in the deal was *Vistafjord* and her sister ship, *Sagafjord*.

Under the name Norwegian America Cruises the two vessels sailed on as cruise liners for nearly three years, but did not at this stage prove as profitable as had been hoped.

In 1983 Trafalgar House, then owner of Cunard, bought the ships and the Norwegian America Cruises business. *Vistafjord* was given a £4.5m refit in Malta and embarked on a career as a Cunard cruise liner.

In April 1997 a blaze broke out in a laundry area aboard *Vistafjord* while she was sailing eastwards across the Atlantic. The lifeboats were swung out and lifejackets donned in readiness as passengers and crew prepared to evacuate the ship. However, this did not prove necessary as the crew managed to put the fire out. Tragically, a steward lost his life through the effects of smoke. Cunard was taken over by Carnival Corporation the following year and in December 1999 the ship was renamed *Caronia* after undergoing a major refit. After a successful career with Cunard, *Caronia* was sold to Saga Cruises in 2003, given a refit and in 2005 entered service as a cruise liner for Saga, her name being changed to *Saga Ruby*.

Swan Hunter's Neptune Yard launched its final vessel in 1988, but Neptune's queen, the former *Vistafjord*, is continuing to win the hearts of passengers as the graceful *Saga Ruby*.

TWAS, Swan Hunter Archive

Farewell! Vistafjord reaches the mouth of the Tyne, poised for her crossing to Norway in May 1973.

Ships (earlier names appear in brackets)

Alfonso XII 34-35

Andania 50

Apollo (Empress of Canada) 54

Apollon (Empress of Canada) 54

Arkadia (Monarch of Bermuda) 39

Ascania 50

Astrid Naess 44

Aurania 50

Ausonia, 50

Baltic 25

Ben Ledi (tug) 19

Bergensfjord 46-49

Berlin (Gripsholm) 45

Bremen 7, 19, 20

Californian 25

Caronia 25

Caronia (Vistafjord) 70

Carpathia 6, 22-33

Cat-Link V 7

Catalonia 7

City of Durban 58

City of Exeter 58

City of Port Elizabeth 58

City of York 58

Conqueror (tug) 19

De Grasse (Bergensfjord) 49

Dominion Monarch 39-43, 52

Empress of Canada 52-54

Empress of England 55

Eugenia Chandris 49

Europa 19

Franconia 64

Gauntlet (tug) 12

Giulio Cesare 62-63

Gloire 67

Golden Moon (Bergensfjord) 49

Great Emperor (tug) 19

Great Western 7

Gripsholm 45

Ivernia 6

Joseph Crosthwaite (tug) 19

Laconia 64

Laconia (second ship of the name) 66-67

Leda 47

Lucky Star (Empress of Canada) 54

Lusitania 6, 7, 14

Master Cat 7

Mauretania 2, 5-21, 25, 52

Mauretania (launched 1938) 21

Meduana 66

Messaba 25

Monarch of Bermuda 36-39

Mongolia 56

Morro Castle 36

New Australia (Monarch of Bermuda) 39

Normandie 7

Northern Star 60-61

Ocean (tug) 10

Ocean Monarch 43-44

Olympic (Empress of Canada) 54

Oslofjord 49

Plover (tug) 19, 21

Poolzee (tug) 10

President (tug) 12

Principe Perfeito 34

Queen Mary 7

Queen of Bermuda 36

Ranchi 56

Ranpura 56-57

Rasa Sayang (Bergensfjord) 49

Reina del Mar (Ocean Monarch) 44

Reina Victoria-Eugenia 2

Rex 7

Saga Ruby (Vistafjord) 70

Sagafjord 70

Sirius 7

Snowdon (tug) 10, 12

Snowdrop 32

Southern Cross 60

Star of Texas (Empress of Canada) 54

Talma 56

Tilawa 56

Titanic 22-33

Tuber Rose (Mauretania) 18

United States 7

Varna (Ocean Monarch) 44

Vistafjord 68-70

Washington (tug) 10, 12, 19